**writings, stories, and
other free associations**

JOEL CARTER

Canukshuk Artworks
2001 East Fouth Street
Duluth, Minnesota 55812
joel_dlh@yahoo.ca

Lava Lamp Lessons: writings, stories, and other free associations

Text and cover photo by Joel Carter
Lava Lamp illustation by Laura Hjelm
Cover and interior design by Tony Dierckins

"Hands" was originally published in the *Los Angeles Times*, March
26, 2001, under the title "A Touch Can Speak Volumes." "An Old
Friend" was orignially published in the *Los Angeles Times*, April 29,
2002, under the title "Her Gift Outlasted Her Life" and also
published in *Readers' Digest*, September, 2002, under the title
"Jocelyn's Gift: A Lesson for Life." "Important Announcement" was
originally published in the *Annals of Emergency Medicine*,
November, 2000, under the same title.

First Edition, 2004

04 05 06 07 08 · 5 4 3 2 1

ISBN: 0-9745847-1-1

Printed in the U.S.A.

Publishing consultation provided by:

www.x-communication.org

For my mom and dad.

— J.C.

My thanks to my therapist for the discounted rates
I've received over the years. Also, my appreciation and
thanks to Rhoda Fukushima, Greg Bernhardt,
June Kallestad, and Tony Dierckins for their red pens,
input, and catching most of my mistakens.

— J.C.

Contents

Preramble

I've always wanted to write a book with a Lava Lamp on the cover. The Lava Lamp on the cover of this book has been with me a long time. I have a special relationship with it—it's worn in and comfortable, like a pair of old jeans. I could have used a new Lava Lamp for the cover shot, but there's just something about a well lit and worn-in Lava Lamp. Lately, I've felt my life has been a bit like a Lava Lamp. In fact, my therapist recently asked me, "If you could choose to be any kind of Lava Lamp, what kind of Lava Lamp would you choose to be, and why." I told her I didn't really care for the "glittery-shimmery" ones. The standard deep violet with yellow lava with black accent base and cap feels right—it seems happy with what it is and well rooted to its base. I'm sure it must relate to something Freudian, but that's a place I don't want to go right now.

My therapist thought that this book project would be a worthwhile exercise of my creative process—a little personal expression to keep me off the streets and channel my obsession for decaffeinated vanilla lattes into something innovative. She assured me that any spelling errors and oversittes would be a good experience and strengthen my personal exceptance of my own imperfections. I thought I should write something about life experiences. I soon realized it was going to be too expensive and inconvenient to write about someone else's life, but that my life experiences would be readily available and cheap. I wouldn't have to put myself on retainer or schedule meetings with myself. I'm getting along well with who I am, so it seemed like the ideal working relationship.

Many pieces for this book were inspired by Lava Lamp moments. I once inverted my old Lava Lamp and saw how it, like life, was full of endless possibilities once it was turned upside down and the large lava forms broke open into myriad forms and fragments.

Many of the pieces in this small contribution of thoughts and stories have been motivated by those types of moments: Lava Lamp Lessons. I've been gathering them for some time now. Most are short and sweet. A few have gone places on their own, visiting the pages of the *Los Angeles Times*, *Readers Digest*, and an academic emergency medicine journal, *Annals* (don't worry, it's not what you think). These are not meant to be profound works of literature, but free flowing associations and compilations of consciousness that have not been intimidated by restrictive form, style, or copy editors. There aren't any real rules for Lava Lamp books. By nature they must be unpredictable and in a constant state of change.

They say you can never judge a book by its cover, but you can be the judge. My therapist said she thought it turned out quite well. I hope you enjoy the stories.

—Joel Carter, 2003

An Old Friend

For Jocelyn

During my first year of medical school, I met an old friend whom I hadn't seen for years. One of my first patients, she was to teach me the most important lesson of my medical training; the magic of story.

The first semester had been full of lengthy, regimented, theory-laden lectures. The topics seemed irrelevant to the daily practice of medicine or to people's lives. I labored under the delusion that I could learn it all, or at least collapse valiantly trying.

As our training progressed, we inched closer to patients. Our textbook assignments and lectures gave way to case scenarios discussed in small groups. We met the patients only as anonymous adults or children referenced by age and gender. We knew nothing about their lives or who they were as people. One afternoon this all changed. Our small group was meeting for our scheduled pathology rounds, looking at the clinical presentations of disease through microscopes or on slides of preserved specimens. It was a beautiful, warm autumn day, and the wind was blowing the last of the leaves from the trees. I was daydreaming of being outside, perhaps going for a run, vaguely aware of the discussion going on in the background.

The Lava Lamp Lessons

Then the class turned to the last case study in our handouts. The patient was a 17-year-old female who had developed knee pain over a few days to weeks. She was diagnosed with osteosarcoma of the femur, one of the most common bone cancers in teens and young adults. Her leg was amputated at the hip in an attempt to save her life. Despite aggressive treatment, she died.

The story sounded familiar. In my thoughts, I was suddenly back at Kelvin High School in Winnipeg, Canada, during the autumn of 1979, my senior year. In the distance I saw the silhouette of a girl at her locker, sorting through her backpack and books. She turned, and I recognized the beaming face of Jocelyn Hutton, a slender brunette with an infectious smile and a magnetic personality. I had not thought of her in years.

The last time I had seen her was several months later, around Christmastime. She had been diagnosed with osteosarcoma. Her leg was gone. She was in a lot of pain, but her smile was just as unforgettable. She had told her father that she believed her vocation was to tell others that it's OK to die. She died a short time after our last visit. The home she lived in is now a hospice known as Jocelyn House, in a lovely, quiet neighborhood of Winnipeg.

Back in the classroom, I opened my eyes, and my attention returned to the slides.

"What year did this case occur?" I asked.

The instructor didn't know. "It must have been years ago," she replied.

My classmates' banter quieted. A few glanced at me, then looked away. I felt a growing unease in the pit of my stomach, and my heart rate quickened.

An Old Friend

The patient's chest X-ray was displayed, showing lungs filled with a tumor that had spread from the leg cancer.

"What's the date on the X-ray?" I asked.

The instructor looked carefully and said, "1979."

The same year Jocelyn was struck by cancer.

I looked up at the screen once again and stared. The instructor advanced the slide projector, and a picture of Jocelyn's cancerous, amputated femur appeared on the screen. Some of my classmates, realizing that the images displayed on the screen had a connection with my past, bowed their heads. I continued to see Jocelyn's face before me as we filed out of the classroom.

I soon found myself out in the concourse by the seminar rooms. I sat by myself, but wasn't alone.

A few minutes passed, and then a classmate approached me. "Joel, who was she?"

"She was a good friend with a beautiful smile," I said.

The gift of Jocelyn's story opened my eyes to people's lives and their enduring legacies in a way my medical studies never did or could. It was a wonderful gift and a special blessing to have my life touched by her again. And I thought that's the best part of what old friends are for—and what stories are all about.

Sweet Corn

For my mom

Nine Lynwood Road is the address of the Old Farm where my grandparents lived in upstate New York, just outside of Peekskill. Just nine acres with a few old buildings and bungalows, the farm was surrounded by fields of sweet corn in the summer when we visited my mother's parents. Daily you could hear blasts from the guns in the fields that would serve to scare the crows. The sound would boom through the branches of that huge old Oak that canopied the house and gravel drive—old wooded yard chairs gathered in back by the open grill. Lazy hammocks hung about the tall grass. The old well was close by with the green pump that was always fun to push and pull under the vines and grapes that hung above. In the evening the grill would be lit and the sweet corn cooked over the fire that I tended as best as a nine-year-old could. When ready, the corn would be dripped in butter and salt. The meals were always relaxing—peaceful—as the corn slowly disappeared and vanished from sight.

I went back to the Old Farm a few years ago. The acres have since been split up by housing developments and partitioned by fences. I walked up the old driveway—the farmhouse with a new addition but otherwise unchanged. I saw the old water pump lying stripped in the bushes, paint peeling off. That old Oak stood still in the centre—wind blowing through the high branches. I went up and touched the trunk like I had done decades ago. A warm wind blew and rustled the memories and feelings of sweet corn a time long ago.

TV Ratings

My unlisted number rang yesterday. It was Mary from
the Nielsen TV rating company contacting me to become a
"Nielsen TV rating" family. I was contacted because I am
"unique" and there is "no one else like me" who
could give them the "information they need."

I said "I'd be happy to help, although there's one problem."
"What's that?" she asked.
"I haven't watched TV since February 1996," I answered.
"Oh," she said, "…that is unique."
She paused for a moment then added, "You know, I don't
watch that much TV either."

Perhaps I'm not that unique after all.

Doggie-Laser-Lock

For Bailey and Paul

I set off recently on my daily walk with my smooth collie Teva. As we strolled down the back lane past my neighbor Paul's house, I was overcome by a sudden weakness—as if caught in some intergalactic tractor beam immobilizing my forward momentum. My gaze was slowly pulled up and to the left where the majestic figure of Paul's rough collie Bailey, Teva's best buddy, was overlooking and staring intently at us through the silver wire fencing enclosing the yard.

Teva stopped. I stopped. Bailey looked at Teva, Teva looked at me, and I looked back at Bailey.

I then began to feel the presence of the two mind-melding canine four-leggeds invading my neuro-synaptic clefts, depleting the neurotransmitter reserves and gaining control of the sodium-potassium intracellular pumps and ionic exchange pathways. Extracellular calcium and neuromuscular fibers began to have multisystem failures in both smooth and striated muscle integrity. Neuronal functioning at higher cortical levels impacting conscious intention became essentially nonexistent. With the complete breaching of the sensory and motor synaptic pathways and other multi-system failures, laryngeal spasms ensued followed by diaphragmatic tonic-clonic contractures. These slowly began to crescendo and grow in intensity until finally a critical threshold was exceeded and out shot from my oropharyngeal structures the sonic explosion of *"Come on, Bailey!"*

Bailey instantly darts toward the gate and soon is down the steps next to Teva as they both turn and trot down the back lane, side by side, toward the creek.

I eventually regain my composure and dutifully try to catch up to the two canine four-leggeds.

That Doggie-Laser-Lock will get you every time.

We Need Help in the Garage

Automatic doors swing wide. Chevy truck with engine hot and off. Passenger door open. Female sprawled over from the cab seats to the front yelling, sweating, and stretched out. *She's having a baby!* How the hell are we going to get her out? No third door when you need it. Legs and torso grabbed and pulled onto stretcher. Trauma Room 2. Jeans off. Head showing. Here we go. *"Boil some water!"*

Obstetrical nurses materialize out of the walls. Gown and gloves would help. Suction ready. Haven't done this for a while. What was the golden rule of Obstetrics? *"Don't drop that baby!"* Pressure on head. Support the perineum. Don't let her tear. That is the head, isn't it? yes, it's the head. "Vertex"—that's the word. Don't let her tear. "Towel please." Support the perineum. Don't let her tear. No meconium. That's good. "OK, push." Head's coming. "Slowly." Don't let her tear. Support. Pressure. "Slowly." "Slowly." Head's out. "Suction." Check neck for wrapped cord. Can't feel cord. Wait. Cord's there. Cord unwrapped. Wait. Another cord loop. Don't tear cord. Unwrapped again. Start pulling downward. Gentle. Get that anterior shoulder out. Don't let her tear. Posterior shoulder's stuck. Pull up. *And there it is! It's a baby!* "It's a boy."

Pretty blue and limp. Start stimulating and drying. Something about ABGAR scores. Can't really remember what. Small cough. Bigger cough. Faint cry. "He's O.K." Something about clamping cord now. Cord clamp materializes out of thin air. "Thanks." Gentle pressure on the cord. "Do you need a cord sample?" Haven't said that in a while. Gentle pressure on the cord. Wait for the placenta to release. Something about inverting the uterus and losing style points. Manual removals suck big time. Wait. Be patient. Not much bleeding. Gentle pressure. There it is, intact. Time to check the perineum. A little bleeding. One clot. Two clots. Check for tears. No tears. *Yes!*

"Nice to meet you both. Congratulations. Oh by the way, my name's Joel."

Charles is now looking pretty pink on Mom's chest. Head's a little wind blown. Eyes blink open once. And then again.

He's alive.

And so am I.

Epilogue

The Emergency Room seems to be the place that gathers into itself life's agonies of trauma, addictive dysfunctions and their consequences, the spiraling end-stages of disease processes and the inescapable reality of aging. Notwithstanding, it is also a place of many beginnings. Sometimes, that's a hard thing to remember. But today...I remembered.

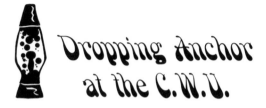

Dropping Anchor at the C.W.U.

In many ways the Emergency department reminds me of a busy shipyard. All types of vessels find their way into port for safe refuge and repair. Some have come under their own steam. A number are tugged into harbor, discovered at sea adrift on the verge of sinking with lack of power and control. Many vessels have minor work done and are quickly sent on their way. Others with serious problems require a number of weeks up in dry docks to be stabilized, refitted and patched. Some will not set sail again, being beyond repair and essentially scrap—if there are any salvageable parts left.

A number of weeks ago I was working the fast track area of our department. Minor complaints, those that aren't "supposed" to take much time, are triaged to keep the flow of patients going. "Minor Complaints" are relative, of course. The time available all depends on how many charts are lined up on the desk, how many patient eyes follow your movements impatiently, whether the nurse helping is having a good day, and when you had your last refueling of coffee.

Early in the shift I saw three patients requesting the Chemical Withdrawal Unit, or C.W.U.. Family brought in the first fellow, Dimitri. He had been drinking the night before. He was in his sixties but looked seventy; tobacco-stained fingers; unshaven face. He had to see a doctor "*right now*" after waiting "*ten minutes.*" As I assessed him for signs of withdrawal, it was obvious that he wanted a quick fix, a "pill" for his nerves, and he would try his best to stay off the sauce.

Tom, a young male in his late twenties, was next. He had long rock-band hair and bilateral bicep tattoos. His tattoo-to-tooth ratio was quite high, a likely predictor of poor outcome with any treatment program. "I can't fuckin' live without alcohol and I'm going to fuckin' die if you don't admit me," he succinctly stated. I've noted that "fuckin'" is the adjective of choice used by young male substance abusers to emphasize the magnitude of their problems. I've actually found a linear relationship between the frequency of use and return visits to the ER. He was admitted. I sensed our paths would cross again soon.

John was the last, an unemployed farmer from rural Manitoba who had trouble with alcoholism for years. He was a plain, chubby man in a flannel jacket and obligatory truck-stop baseball cap. Unmarried with no family, he had gotten a ride with a friend to be seen in a "city" hospital. I asked him about himself and his story. At the end of my questions he sat back and simply but sincerely asked, "Can you help me?" John's day of reckoning had come.

It seems people have to be brought to a "time and space" by events that strip our defenses and force one to that quiet place of reckoning. I looked up the word "reckoning." It's actually a nautical term relating to the calculation of a ship's position based on the stars. It makes sense that before we set sail it's important to know where we came from and how we got to where we are. For many of us, whatever forces us to drop anchor and self reflect could be the best thing to ever happen. I thought that John dropping anchor at the C.W.U. was a perfect example. I'm sure we'll all come to a point of wondering where life is headed one day or another. At that time, stopping to take our bearings from the stars may not be such a bad idea.

 Lava Lamp Lessons

I've kept my lava lamp on for the last few days.
The violet lava slowly danced in large flowing forms.
I went up to the lamp today and turned it over.
The large forms broke open and an infinite
number of particles flowed within.

I stared with wonder and thought that life
is filled with endless possibilities.

Before they're revealed, however, our world
sometimes needs to be turned upside down.

 Crazy Boy

"What's your name, kid?" I asked.

"They call me Crazy Boy," he said.

"Why Crazy Boy?"

"Because I'm Robin Williams with twist."

"With a twist. How so?"

"Because I spin."

"Show me."

And he got up from the chair.
And he spun and he spun and
he spun. And then he laughed
and he laughed and he laughed.

After that—
I decided
I would start
spinning too.

 # Transcendence, Transformation, & Hockey

For Scott

I had a recent exchange with my friend Scott, who expressed concerns regarding two hours of ice time for a recent Old Timer Hockey game. He questioned the extended time commitment and the need to double dose his thyroid supplement in order to participate. Obviously, he wasn't aware of the deeper aspects of the game, self-evident to those steeped in its tradition. In what follows I express the essence of hockey as a resource for self-inquiry and enlightenment. I had no choice—I'm Canadian.

Scott—you need to appreciate that hockey is a sacred art form practiced in the same fashion as the ancient Japanese Green Tea Ceremony. Subtle rituals taken in isolation represent only one aspect of the encounter. In the context of the totality of the experience, true awareness and pure being is attained. Some call this "Nirvana," "Buddha consciousness." Gaining knowledge and wisdom that the journey can only be grasped by action and not by contemplation alone.

Let me review the Twelve-Step Hockey Program so you may better appreciate the time requirement.

The Lava Lamp Lessons

1. The Drive to the Arena

The initial point of focus for the initiating event—the step of commitment that sets the foundation of the group experience and gathering ceremony.

2. Entering the Dressing Room

Crossing the threshold and entering into the "clearing space." Here you will learn a new vernacular and sense primal emanations that stir the warrior within. Tribal chanting greets each solo practitioner and marks assimilation into the whole. At this point one senses the true task at hand. Thoughts of fear and self-doubt are commonplace. Do not be afraid. Learn to make fear your friend.

3. Taping the Stick

The stick symbolically represents the masculine energies and humankind's procreational life force. Self-care on the ice begins with self care of the stick. Taping the stick being central to good puck control and a worthy +/- average. Torching and bending the fiberglass elements of the blade's curve to maximize transfer of energy. Mindful of the potential for an illegitimate stick and subsequent two-minute penance in the penalty box.

4. Stepping on the Ice—The Transformation

Moving from one plane of our connection with the earth and ourselves to another. Stepping off the solid walkway and onto the vast white sheet of ice. Walking on water in its altering form metaphorically imprints the interface between different levels of personal consciousness and physical velocity. Remember to have your skates sharpened and double knot your laces!

5. The Stretch — The Warmup

The preparatory phase in which kinetic maneuvers aid the mind-body continuum and concrescence. Deepening one's awareness and limits of our physicality, especially of the focused areas of the hip flexors, abductors, and collateral ligaments. Remember the ibuprofen!

6. The Skills and Agility Contests

Actual confrontation with our shadow selves and adversarial alter egos who will no doubt attempt to controvert the true essence of who you are. The task is to become rooted and contained—flexible and bending in the wind of adversity—yet maintaining stability and the puck on your stick at all costs. The stick held firm as life force and creative spirit. The puck represents the darkness of the infidel opponents. You'll know intuitively what to do with your stick and how to "handle" the puck.

7. The Face-Off

Entering the void. The dropping of the puck marks the point of no return and complete surrender to the process. It also signals the starting line-up to simultaneously drop the gloves—throwing off the shackles and restrictive elements and engage completely into the first forceful connection (A.K.A. the "bench clearing brawl"). Remember, facemasks are for weinies and soft-styled European hockey teams sponsored by JOFA!

8. The Penalty Box

Accepting the invitation into the inner sanctum by the higher authority. Opportunity for quiet self-reflection and solitude from the collective. A time-out for short-termed vision questing and refocusing in the midst of hostile chanting and Budweiser baptisms from the gathered assemblage.

9. The Play—Beyond the Threshold

The give and take of life's journey mirrors the team play. The puck is a shared experience. Striking a balance between possession and "letting go." The ultimate objective being success of the collective. Finding the optimal locale to receive, accept, internalize, and then blasting the incarnate black rubber mass right through the bloody five hole! Remember, their goalie is a sieve on low shots.

10. The Final Minute

Realizing near completion of the inner journey and the spent competitive spirit while awaiting the final whistle. Last ditch efforts and pulling the goalie for a sixth attacker for the final barrage. Mindfully present in the pounding of the infidel opponents into absolute submission—with compassion, mercy and loving-kindness.

11. State of Joy

The final whistle segues to physical collapse and joy. A point at which we all come to personal terms with our limitations, yet equally balanced with the ecstasy of physical dominance, victory, and pure state of being-ness. This also entails the end of the game handshake. Coming together as brothers and reconciling in view of the cheap shots doled out in the corners—out of eye shot of the referee.

12. Purging

Receiving the post-game offerings and cleansing sacraments. Re-establishing hydrational and electrolyte balance, the metabolism of lactate, and maintaining good perfusion of the kidneys in light of the physical and psychic demands of the experience. Urine dip-sticks will be available post-game to identify any absence of myogobinuria amongst the collective. If you don't pee blood—you held back—and the journey needs to be repeated.

⌇

So there you have it, Scott, in a nutshell. Oh yeah—remember your jock! A little synopsis of what hockey is really about on the deeper levels. As you may now envision and appreciate, two hours on the ice reflects a lifetime of experience. Taken as a whole, if you were to reduce all this down to one take-home message, I think it maybe is this—your extra thyroid supplement is a crutch and ain't gonna help you a damn with this one!

 Teva

I feed her bits of Angus beef steak
and she eats her shit if I'm not fast enough.

I get "doggie-going" in the morning
with micro-waved food bowl
and biscuit aperitif.

She companionizes me as we
trail down creek rocks and up
into the thick bush overlooking the city.

She does well for five or six
Frisbee air grabs and then gets bored—
"time to sniff and mark" she seems to say,
and I mind less she's collie and not retriever.

She's a herding dog and tends to
lag on the late night walks.
After a sauna I get my "cleaning"
as she licks the salt off my back and face.

Once, I looked into her eyes
and the expanse of the universe
looked back at me.

And that's why I feed her steak.

 Training

During a recent skipping workout I
watched a lean and fierce female in her
forties work a "heavy bag" blow after
blow for some time.

At the right moment I asked, "What are you
training for?" And without missing a beat
and in perfect cadence she said, "Life."

I realized then—that's what
I've been training for too.

 Solo

I decided to give myself clearance to
fly my life solo for some time to come.
It wasn't the most stylish take-off
but I managed to get the landing gear up.

I radio'ed the tower to tell them
I was doing O.K.—and didn't have any
particular heading in mind. The said
I'd have good visibility after
breaking through the cloud ceiling.

So I pulled back on the stick and headed up
through some dense cloud cover.

As I broke through, the sun was on the
western horizon and a beautiful sea of
white extended beyond what my eyes could see.
Blue skies were above with high wisps of
some cirrus clouds.

Thought I'd continue to gain some elevation and
garner some breath-taking views and perspectives.

Might even try some maneuvers, open it up,
and see what this baby can do....

# Important Announcement

Good evening, ladies and gentlemen. This is Dr. Carter speaking to you from the central Control Island here in the emergency department. I'd like to take this opportunity on behalf of all ED staff to welcome and thank you for choosing our ED and trauma center for your acute health care needs. We are anticipating a full ED tonight, so in order to facilitate treatment plans, we will be initiating assessments by strict triage criteria. Please have your health plan cards readily available. This is a preoperative announcement only. We will begin general examinations shortly. Those patients with preferred "cash" pay plans, a first-degree relative in the health care profession, or a special "Middle Eastern Kingdom Care" account can make your way to the treatment rooms at your convenience. Again, this is a preoperative announcement only.

We would now like to invite individuals with the following symptoms to enter the treatment area: sudden-onset headache with an episode of loss of consciousness, ripping pain in the upper back with radiation into the chest, and right upper or lower quadrant pain associated with fever, rigors, and recurrent vomiting. Also, those noting heavy bleeding of bright red blood from the vagina or rectum or having black, tarry-colored stools associated with a pale complexion can enter the treatment area at this time. A trauma surgeon certified by the American College of Surgeons will assess individuals with trauma involving two systems or more. All medical staff involved in trauma care have been fully credentialed with ATLS and have attained 18 hours credit of continuing medical education specific in trauma as per strict ACS guidelines.

On completion of primary surveys and initial workups, we will then ask those with the following vital signs to make your way to the examination rooms. Individuals with systolic blood pressures greater than 250 or less than 70 mm Hg, regular or irregular heart beats greater than 150 or less than 40 beats/min, respiratory rates greater than 40 or less than six breaths/min, and rectal temperatures of greater than 40 degrees C or lower than 34 degrees C may enter the examination area. Patients with complete absence of vital signs may be bumped to another holding facility dependent on downtime. Please do not enter the treatment area unless your vital sign has been called.

To begin assessments, we need all patients in their beds with the bed rails in the upright and locked position and with the ECG leads securely fastened. According to federal regulations, the area immediately around the bed must be completely clear of personal belongings. These articles may be stowed directly underneath the stretcher or in the personal belonging bags that our health care attendants would be happy to tag and stow for you. We also request that all patients upon entering the ED turn off any cell phones, televisions, or radios as these may interfere with automatic defibrillators, pacemakers, and life support equipment.

I would now like to direct your attention to the nurse

anesthetist and respiratory technician for an important demonstration. In the unlikely event of loss of airway reflexes or respiratory drive, an oral airway will descend from above you and be inserted into your oral cavity and pharynx. A flow of 100 percent oxygen will commence, and you will be manually bagged until your respiratory drive and reflexes normalize or until definitive airway management is attained through endotracheal intubation. We ask you to please refrain from aspirating immediately before, during, or after the procedure.

This JCAHO-compliant ED and trauma center is part of an integrated health care system, fully equipped with an all-encompassing service-line approach, mission statement, peer review process, and quality initiatives. There are also a total of three washrooms in the department: one in the fast-track section and two in the ED. Each is equipped with smoke detectors and point-of-service urine drug screen kits. It is a federal offense to tamper with, disable, or destroy the smoke detectors or to adulterate your urine or submit an erroneous sample. Punishment is by way of, but not limited to, gastric lavage with an Ewald tube or soapsuds enema through a rectal tube.

A call button has been conveniently clipped to your hospital gown. We would appreciate you pushing the call button should you experience any recurrent chest pain, severe shortness of breath with air hunger, or simply a general sense of impending doom. Your examination room has been stocked with a number of kidney basins should you experience any vomiting. Please take a moment now to locate the nearest kidney basin, remembering that the nearest kidney basin may be the one directly behind you.

The Lava Lamp Lessons

We would also like to take this opportunity to welcome back our frequent flyers and thank you for choosing us again to service all your all your narcotic addiction and withdrawal needs. For your own safety and comfort, as well as for the safety and comfort of those addicts seated around you, we ask you to please keep your intravenous needles capped throughout the duration of your assessment, especially if you feel the need to move about the ED to steal prescription pads and raid drug stocks.

For those exhibiting symptoms of psychosis, paranoia, or delusions, we'd be pleased to administer an appropriate dose of the neuroleptic of your choosing. For a complete list of your medication options, please consult the *PDR* manual located on the table directly beside your bed.

Shortly, we will be coming through the ED offering your hydration and fluid resuscitation with the intravenous fluid of your choice. Tonight, we are featuring either Ringer's lactate with 20 mEq/L KC1 or D5W with 100 mg of thiamine and an amp of bicarbonate. We would appreciate your understanding should we run out of your preference at the time of your intravenous start.

For patients actively experiencing upper or lower gastrointestinal bleeding of bright red blood, there have been some delays in clearing the endoscopic suite. We expect this to be rectified in the next sixty minutes. We will keep you informed as more information is made available. For those of you interested with lower gastrointestinal bleeding, the colonscopy course should take us initially due north through the rectum, deviating somewhat through the sigmoid colon. The upward course will then continue through the descending colon, curving through the splenic flexure and up across the transverse colon. At the hepatic flexure, the scope will change to a downward direction and continue on until arrival at its final destination, the cecum.

As a special feature tonight in the ED, all patients presenting with urethral or vaginal discharge will be awarded a pharmaceutical voucher for an intramuscular injection of Rocephin and a seven-day course of doxycline. This voucher is redeemable at the pharmacy of your choosing and meets JCAHO guidelines for medication sample distribution.

Once again, ladies and gentlemen, thank you for choosing our ED and trauma center for your acute care needs. We do realize you have a choice in health care, and we appreciate your business. If there is anything else we can do to make your ED visit more enjoyable, please do not hesitate to push your call button, and we will respond as best we can. On behalf of myself and all members of this fully credentialed ED staff, we'd like to wish you good health and stable vital signs whatever your final procedure or operation may be. Now sit back, relax, and enjoy your intervention. The local time is approximately 8:40 P.M. Charge nurse and team leaders prepare for patients. Cross-match and on call.

 # Warrior Wound

I had some acid spill and scar my right arm
some time ago. I showed the scar to a friend.
She said it's my "warrior wound" and that
our wounds are maps to the soul.

I think she's right.

I also know it hurt quite a lot
and took a long time to heal.

 # Kite Flying

I went out and flew a kite for the first
time at age 37. The wind seized the wings
and it streamed up into the sky. I tried some
loops and after some time I lost control. The
kite came down hard and the frame snapped.

A new lateral spar arrived a few weeks later
and I restored the broken section.

It's ready to go again.

Can't be scared to try again after
losing control and getting all bent out of shape.

The Starbucks Coffee-Club Lady Dialogues

Part I: The Purge

Some time ago, I decided to leave the caffeinated world behind and see what decaf life was all about. I thought purging myself of years of caffeine might give some new perspective and a purer sense of self-reliance and honest inner limitations.

So, I called 1-800-STARBUCKS. After two rings, a pleasant female voice answered. "Thank you for calling the Starbucks Coffee Company and Support Center. How can I help you?" She had a calming way about her and said she was the Starbucks Coffee-Club Lady.

I told her that I was going through some major life changes and was on the threshold of some undiscovered territory of my own deep intra-psychic structures. I told her that I wanted to break out of old dysfunctional patterns and move into a newer conscious relationship with myself.

She said that she rarely gets requests for emerging levels of consciousness—especially from males—but would be happy to help in any way she could, apparently having been there herself a number of years ago.

I took a deep breath, exhaled slowly, and asked her to switch me to decaf blends. She suggested that I order some peppermint and wild raspberry herbal teas. I thought I should order some newly designed coffee and tea brewing systems to serve as a focus for my percolating inner processes.

She wished me luck, and said that she would be available any time I wanted to talk—just give her a call.

So far I'm doing OK. My withdrawal headaches are gone. Friends tell me I'm more settled and calm. I seem to be more focused and present. I'm trying to get more in touch with my feelings and deeper levels of awareness. Otherwise, the only thing I've noticed is that I'm slammin' a can of Pringles a day.

I'm sure everything is going to be OK.

Part II: The Abyss

My decaf coffee reserves ran out this morning. Starbucks held my last shipment due to a new expiratory date on my Visa card.

I found a half-full bag of Cafe Verona tucked away in the back of the freezer—the caffeinated kind, a full-bodied blend with aromatic richness, a creamy smooth textured elixir with a hint of cinnamon. So I had a cup.

It was only one cup.

OK, it was what "some people" would call a "Grande" size—a fairly large portion, but it's all relative.

I feel fine. I'm a little tachycardic and got a little bit of a buzz, but it ain't nothin' I can't handle. I'm still the same person. I'm still able to make conscious choices in my life. It isn't like I've jumped into the abyss or anything like that. I mean, what was I supposed to do? After all, it wasn't my fault the shipment was delayed. It was *their* fault.

The Starbucks Coffee Club Lady should have anticipated circumstances like this happening and not abandon their "valued customers," leaving them in the dark and decaffeinatedless.

And what's the point of having "expiration dates" on credit cards, anyways? It only screws up deliveries and shipments when everything was working just fine—thank you very much! I wonder if *American Express* has "expiration dates" on their cards.

It was only one cup!

Part III: Clarification

My delayed decaffeinated blends finally arrived from Starbucks, and not a moment too soon. They threw in a complimentary half bag of their decaf "Holiday Blend" in appeasement. Obviously they want to keep me as a valued customer—happy and satisfied.

So I called the Starbucks Coffee Club Lady to get some feedback regarding this "happy and satisfied" stuff. I thought, who better to get counsel from when coming to grips with the metamorphosis of a caffeinated paradigm to a decaf awakening. Surely she should have some sagacity.

She asked me what I really wanted. "To be happy and satisfied," I said.

She said that to be truly happy, one needs to look at what "caffeinated" and "decaffeinated" really represent at her or his deeper intra-psychic structures. She went on to outline how caffeine can become concretized and take on "shadow" qualities pertaining to both feminine and masculine archetypal energies. The task at hand becomes one of acceptance and integrating one's shadow. Within the soul's crucible or "grinder," holding the tension of the opposites creates an opportunity for a third form to manifest—the True Self.

She said I was on the right path and would intuitively know how to proceed. She also recommended the Blue Note Decaf Blend for my next order and then had to go to attend the next customer.

I hung up the phone, settled back and reflected for some time on her words. Then, quietly, from a place deep within, I felt the voice of the inner masculine speak. I then knew how to proceed.

I went to the 'fridge, cracked open a beer, and sat down to watch the football game on TV. I'd worry about my "True Self" at half-time.

"Ball's on the thirty-five—third down and long!"

Somewhere even deeper in my intra-psychic structure, I sensed the voice of the inner feminine scream in defiant agony, "We've got a *long* way to go!"

Part IV: Integration

I let the words of the Starbucks Coffee Club Lady regarding "acceptance and integration" percolate for some time. It's no easy task to attempt to integrate "caffeinated" and "decaffeinated" archetypal patterns. I wasn't sure how to proceed, but simply waited and trusted the process.

It seemed I would have to honor and accept both the caffeinated and decaffeinated shadow sides of my deeper intra-psychic structures. Neither to deny nor indulge, but to find the middle way symbolically. So I made my way down to the local Starbucks. I ordered both a caffeinated and decaffeinated Grande

Latte and sat down determined to integrate in the corner booth—
out of earshot of the cashier.

I centered myself by drawing deep breaths in and out. I let go of
all distractions. The rich full-bodied aroma of the lattes filled my
lungs. My breath followed the sweetness of the generous nutmeg
topping with which I had doused the drinks. After some time I had
entered into the non-ordinary state of consciousness necessary to
enhance my ceremonial intention.

I gave thanks and honored the caffeinated and decaffeinated
elements, and then decanted both into a third container from which
I drank.

What happened next is hard to describe. I became aware that
the aroma continued to grow in intensity and evolved into a
sweetness that I had never smelled before. Each breath of the
incense filled my inner aspects completely and induced patterns of
euphoria and well-being not known in my life. Emotional released
welled up with sounds and emanations stemming deep within my
being—almost like the sounds of a universal language that my body
knew but I had forgotten long ago.

After some time the vivid experience began to release me and
quietly resolve. I felt at peace, sedate, and fully integrated.

Slowly, other murmurs began to make their presence known.
Their sounds seemed far away, but became more charged. Then,
with clearing clarity, I heard, "Get an accucheck! I'll start the IV!
Amp of D50 *stat!* He's got a pulse. Steady. Good color. Turn him on
his side! Sir! Sir! Wake up! Wake up!"

I opened my eyes and returned fully from my integrating
experience. Above me were two paramedics—the first shoving a

huge needle into my left arm, the other wrapping a stiff collar around my neck and put me on oxygen. The cashier stood beside them looking panicked.

"Sir, you've had a seizure. Be completely still. We're taking you to hospital. Are you on any medications?" asked the paramedic.

After a CT scan of my head, an EEG, baseline blood work, and four hours of observation, I was discharged from the Emergency Room. The Emergency Physician on duty said my seizure was likely a result of a combination of factors, including hyperventilation, excessive nutmeg exposure, and a lower seizure threshold in the face of caffeine withdrawal symptoms.

I tried to explain to him that I was only trying to integrate my deeper intra-psychic structures.

He said, "Sonny, if you're going to be doing that kind of stuff, you need proper supervision." Then he made an appointment for me with the outpatient Psychiatric Crisis Unit for 9:30 A.M. the next day.

So ended the integrating peak experience of my caffeinated and decaffeinated archetypal energies. I left the Emergency Room that night and meandered home somewhat dazed, disillusioned, and with a major co-pay because of the ambulance ride. What will the Starbucks Coffee Club Lady say when she hears about this?

Part V: New Beginnings

I called the Starbucks Coffee Club Lady to report on my progress. I wanted to let her know that I was doing well and more integrated than ever before. Both the caffeinated and decaffeinated aspects of my deeper intra-psychic structures were fully assimilated. I was now able to live in both caffeinated and decaffeinated worlds consciously—with awareness, boundaries, and the ability to make choices from an authentic perspective: my True Self. Notwithstanding, I also learned my True Self should avoid excess nutmeg in combination with deep centering breathing practices—one trip to the ER was enough.

As I asked to speak to the Starbucks Coffee Club Lady, a guy named Stewart answered and said she was no longer available. She apparently had taken a last-minute sabbitical to a Club Med resort in Cancun, and wasn't scheduled to be back for the foreseeable future.

Initially, I was devastated. I felt my early abandonment issues begin to fire and a pervasive fear of loss settle deep. Stewart was no help here; he couldn't connect with what I was experiencing.

He asked me if I wanted to place an order. I didn't know what to say, but after a few moments I said that I thought it would be best to just cancel my account for now. I said it had nothing to do with the product or the service—"It's just where I am." Stewart said he understood, and thanked me for being a loyal Starbucks Coffee Club member.

After a few minutes, I began to feel better and uplifted. I made myself a cup of coffee—a cup of *caffeinated* Café Verona. It was a good cup of coffee and I drank it slow. I was grateful to the Starbucks Coffee Club Lady and her gifts of insight and wisdom. I wished her the best and wondered where life's journey might take her. In some ways it could be a new beginning for both of us, moving with whatever direction the winds blow. Without endings, there can't be any new beginnings. And with that, I savored the last drops in the cup.

Part VI:
"American Woman" and the Starbucks Coffee Club Lady

I hadn't spoken to the Starbucks Coffee Club Lady for some time, and wondered if she might be back from her sabbatical. I hoped I could connect with her and touch base to check under the hood to see how my intra-psychic structures were doing. You can never be too careful—a regular intra-psychic check-up as well as good dental hygiene can keep you out of trouble.

So, I dialed 1-800-STARBUCKS and asked if she was back from her sabbatical.

They put me on hold and background music began to play. First, it was Barry Manilow's "Mandy," then Billy Joel's "Uptown Girl," followed by "YMCA" by the Village People. I was beginning to get into it when the first few bars of "American Woman" by the Guess Who began to play—the music was cut off, and the Starbucks Coffee Club Lady came on the line.

I was a little nervous, and stuttered a bit, wondering if she'd remember.

"Hi. Remember me?" I said. "I'm the guy you helped through that tough transition from the caffeinated performance-based world view paradigm to a new and formative decaffeinated perspective."

"Of course I do. I've often wondered whatever happened to you. So, how's it going?" she asked.

"Well—I'm more in touch with my feelings and my so-called feminine—stuff. I try to embrace all the moments I can remember. Wanting to continue to stay in my integrity while allowing the paradox and mystery to exist in alignment with the higher good of my soul and those that I encounter along the journey. It's not always easy to learn from my heart instead of my head. Life becomes more and more shades of gray, more than any shade of black or white. If I begin to look, I can see more deeply that I ever imagined. Love and compassion continue to be the greatest teachers of mine in the midst of listening and dancing with those that show up—the dance of which can be pure joy and rapture.

"My friends and family mark the deep treasure chest of my life. All the while I feel there remains even greater depth of self-discovery and wholeness yet to be revealed when the time is right, and emergence is safe. My dog licks my face every day. A good burger is hard to find—but once found is even better with mustard and onions (and a little chocolate raspberry truffle ice cream on the side). I continue not to smoke, but inhale daily from the source. I have forgotten how to plan every day out, and instead wait for the daily moments to lead the way. There's nothing more beautiful than seeing a smile and eyes that sparkle and recognize who you are at the core, instead of looking at what you do and how you act. Allowing myself to be taken care of by those who love me is teaching me how to love myself. Life is short and I'm not here for a long time—as my mom says—'we're all just temps down here.' I've stopped expecting my parents to be what I needed, and I'm trying to let them be who they are.

"There are truly no chance encounters, but only lessons and gifts that are sometimes hard to understand. It's OK to have all my feelings. Time does heal. Everyone has their own stuff, and allowing them to have it is part of allowing them to be responsible for themselves. Knowing where I start and where I end allows others to do the same. Holding on and letting go is part of the deal of being alive—knowing how and when is another story. Death is really just a transformative experience of consciousness and a shedding of a skin that's no longer needed. I never thought I'd be where I am today, and God forbid I should ever know what I'm doing or where I may end up."

There was silence on the other end of the phone. The dial tone hadn't clicked on, and I heard breathing on the other end. "Hello…?" I said.

"My…you seem to have learned a lot these last few years," the Starbucks Coffee Club Lady said quietly. And then, after a pause— "Do you know enough now, to know what you still need to learn?"

Deep down somewhere where "knowing" resides—the answer didn't come, because it was already there.

"Forgiveness," I said.

"And the hardest part to learn will be forgiving yourself," she said.

"I know. I don't know how to do that yet."

"I suspect, someday soon—you will know that too."

There was a long silence on the phone again.

Seems that everything that needed to be said had been said. Yet we both hung on the line with just our breathing interrupting the occasional static and the distant tune of an FM radio station in the background playing Natalie Cole's "Unforgettable."

Hard to hang the phone up sometimes when the connection is so present and strong—but another customer was waiting to place an order, and my time was up. I placed an order for my two pounds of Café Verona—decaf, of course—and said good-bye.

The Starbucks Coffee-Club Lady Dialogues

I thanked the Starbucks Coffee Club Lady, as I always do. It's always wonderful to connect with her. She's quite an amazing woman, wherever she is. I often wonder what she's doing working for Starbucks, but then again, we all gotta do what we gotta do.

I hope I'll get the chance to meet her someday to share a cup of coffee or just hum a beautiful melody. She's probably a lot closer than I think.

Hawk Ridge

I've been running this area of Duluth that overlooks Lake Superior for the past six years now. It's located on the eastern edge of the city, and right in the path of migrating hawks and eagles. I have usually run the front gravel road that climbs gradually up and overlooks the wide expanse of the lake, or have chosen the well-trodden "back side" snowmobile-fire road. I have never ventured into the intervening forest, either due to habit or just because of the added distance of an already long run.

A few weeks ago I drove out and parked at one of the entrance points to the trailhead, and began seeing what I could find as far as the internal trail system that I have suspected existed.

It was a wonderful experience, finding this vast amount of undiscovered country that was between my two familiar routes and I have observed how I've "felt" exploring the new territory—not being familiar with "where things are going" or "where the trail is supposed to be," and with a little trepidation of getting lost in uncharted territory. I've had to do some bushwhacking here and there. I have been off the beaten path, have stumbled across a number of linked trails, and have had to turn around numerous times and backtrack to find my way out or to just check my bearings. I've been to new lookout vistas that have given me new perspective on the surrounding city and the lake, and have found the highest point of Hawk Ridge and some of the entrance points of the trails that I've passed by for years, but never noticed they were there, or was curious enough to explore.

It seems to me to be a metaphor for the inner journey. What are the fears? Why do we pass by these internal trail entrances that go unnoticed for years or decades? What motivates one about setting out and exploring in the first place?

And then the thought came to me about leadership, but from a personal perspective, and framed the question of how does one's own leadership relate to one's own life and the choices that one makes about which trail we follow? Do we turn left or right? And what about the actual decision making processes that we utilize. What or who shaped them, and by what experiences?

I think in relationship with others, arising issues will lead one to the trail head places in our own lives. But I think it is a personal and private solitary experience—this bushwhacking, backtracking of self-discovery, of one's own inner deep forest. It really is a journey into the unknown, the unfamiliar. It comes with risk, but also with opportunities for discovery on top of higher ground.

The Gift of Goodbye

For Mark

I pushed the button to open the automatic doors at the Emergency Room at St. Mary's Hospital in Duluth Minnesota, and made my way past the central workstation to the doctors' office to change for the beginning of my shift.

This night, the usually energetic and boisterous staff was subdued. I figured it was a "bad outcome case." I picked up my stethoscope and pinned on my nametag to my scrub top. Medical problems we see in the emergency room often provoke profound changes for patients and their families—and sometimes unexpected good-byes.

This time, the profound change and unexpected goodbye was ours.

Dan Campbell, the ER physician who I was relieving, walked into the doctor's office and closed the door behind him. "I have some terrible news about Mark," he said.

Mark Rathke, our colleague and medical director, had been at a conference in Florida with his family. At lunch, he had a subarachnoid hemorrhage—a ruptured blood vessel in his brain. Mark had such a gentle demeanor about him that he never had a patient complaint in ten years. Always subtle, understated, and a bit shy, he was forgiving when the rest of us did. He was now in an intensive care unit somewhere in Florida. It did not look good.

"He may not make it," Dan said. "It's going to be a hard shift."

I sat there for sometime, unable to move or think or even cry.

But patients were waiting to be seen. As if on automatic pilot, my training took over and my body found its way to the queued up patient chart rack. Exam room four—someone with abdominal pain. I ordered some blood work and an ultrasound to check for gall bladder problems. Then, a little girl with a sore throat. I wrote a prescription for antibiotics. Exam room one—a patient with serious chest pain. I ordered tests and treatments for a potential heart attack.

We waited for word of Mark's status. Then the phone finally rang. Shelly, our health unit coordinator, answered the phone. We all stopped and watched in silence.

"St. Mary's Emergency Room," she said.

She didn't say anything for sometime. Tears began to well up in her eyes. We all knew Mark had died.

"Thank you for calling," she finally said, and hung up the phone.

All that was composed and contained in the staff finally broke open and overflowed in tears and sorrow. Work ground to a halt as we all began to grieve. No one could function. Thankfully, patients already in the full ER were stable and resting. Incoming ambulances were diverted to other local hospitals. We migrated to the central workstation and together sat and wept.

Twelve minutes amazingly passed without any phone calls, radio transmissions, or any change in the patients under our care.

Then abruptly, the doors of the department swung open and a father carrying his young daughter broke the solemn silence.

"She's having a bad asthma attack," he yelled.

"Put her in exam room three," I said to the nurses while I reached for my stethoscope, "and call Respiratory therapy for some Ventolin breathing treatments!"

I slowly rose and walked toward the father and daughter as the nurses directed them to the examination stretcher. Shelly moved back to her station and placed the call. The other nurses stood, and after a few moments made their way back to check on the other patients. The ER that Mark had directed for nearly a decade slowly wound back up to life. As if in defiance of his death, we all went back to work as best we could.

Later, we learned more details of how Mark died. During one of the conference breaks, he went back to his hotel room where his wife and son were waiting. He opened the door, went inside and sat down on the bed. He visited for some time with his wife Margo, son Sam, and Sam's friend who was with them. After a few minutes, he said, "I gotta go" and said good-bye.

On his way out the door, a small blood vessel in his brain broke, and he collapsed.

Years later, I still often think of that small blood vessel. It seemed to have all the time in the world to decide when to weaken and rupture. In some ways—it seemed to know exactly what it was doing. In a universe that is so arbitrary and unpredictable, that little blood vessel—in its precise timing—gave Mark the gift of being able to say good bye. The hard part was that the rest of us wanted the same chance.

The Magic Menorah

I sat before the Menorah
with the nine candles
waiting.

I had a sense that my
roots were now about
something new as
opposed to something
old.

There hasn't been
a Menorah in my
family for years—
perhaps generations.

In the glow of
lights of the Christmas Tree
I lit the first candle.

Seemed to be
one of those
big medicine
moments.

When I came
back to the
room a little
while later
there were now
two candles
burning.

I smiled and before
I even wondered—
I knew who had lit
the second candle.

 # Take Me Home

Big Dan paced back and forth in Exam Room #14 at the end of the hall. Two security guards stood watch a few feet away. Exam Room #14 is usually reserved for the "disturbed" patients: the psychotic, depressed, or intoxicated. In addition to being moderately intoxicated, Big Dan had a bright red river of blood running down his face from a long gash in his scalp. Three small ponds of congealed blood pooled on the floor. Many of my Emergency Room colleagues rather avoid Exam Room #14, with its downtrodden and belligerent patient profiles; poor "clinical substrate," one partner once voiced. I rather like Exam Room #14 and its cast of characters; they always teach me something about life, and I'm often surprised by the daily lessons. I grabbed the chart and walked in past the security guards, tiptoeing carefully so as not to disturb or slip on Big Dan's hemoglobin mosaic on the floor.

"Doc! Doc! Just send me home! I wanna go home, Doc! Please let me go home. Don't send me to Detox, Doc! Just let me go home," he said as I entered the room and introduced myself. I shook his hand and sized up how many stitches would be needed to close the gash. He wasn't sure how he got the cut, or didn't want to tell me. Maybe a fall. Maybe a fist. Or maybe Big Dan connected with a beer bottle in a distinctive physical manner courtesy of an offended compatriot. It happened down at the Kozy Bar, a vile little establishment in the city core known for its cheap beer, colorful patrons, and frequent 911 phone calls. The police seem to run a shuttle service some nights from the Kozy to the ER, en route to the Detox Center across the street. Big Dan was their most recent drop-off before they headed back for more.

"So, Dan, how much did you drink tonight?" I asked.

"Oh, just a couple," he burped.

"A couple" in the vernacular of Exam Room #14 patients translates to a blood alcohol level at least four times the legal limit. I positioned Dan on the stretcher, made sure he wasn't seriously injured, and began to work on repairing the gaping cosmetic defect. "Do you want me to freeze the cut, Dan?" I offered. "Naaaahhh Doc…just *do it!*" his response came from under the sterile towels.

I began to pass the sutures through his scalp without so much as a flinch. "So Doc…are ya gonna send me home? Come on, Doc! Just let me go home!" he implored. His repeated pleas continued for some time and then made a crescendoing transmutation to the words and familiar music of John Denver: "Take me home…/ Country Roads…/ To the Place…/ I Belong…." I had to hand it to Big Dan—he was pretty good. So good, in fact, that I was moved to join in on the next chorus, as my suturing and repair work continued. And we both sang out together (and in surprisingly good harmony, I might add):

> *Take me home, country roads,*
> *To the place, I belong.*
> *West Virginia, Mountain Mama,*
> *Take me home, country roads.*

Take Me Home

Screams, profanities, and performances that rival the World Wrestling Federation productions usually emanate from Exam Room #14. Our duet, dramatic in a somewhat different manner, elicited a whole host of responses seldom seen in the ER. The two security guards a few feet away began to tap their feet and joined in. Nurses wanting to see what the commotion was left their posts to peer in and hum along. Upset infants and children appeared to calm and settle in their parents' arms, and the ringing phones went unanswered for the short time that this spontaneous ER ensemble was in full voice. Incoming sirens appeared to fade into the distance as the words and melody of "Take me home…" echoed throughout the examination rooms and halls of the emergency department. And as if on cue, the last bars were sung, the final suture was tied in place, and a brief still ness hung in the air as the music faded.

I removed the sterile towel. Beneath was the beaming face of Big Dan glowing in the aftermath of an exhilarating but brief musical odyssey:

"So Doc…are yazz gonna send me home?"

I thought about it for a moment or two, weighed the reasonable options, and replied, "You know, Dan, I really like John Denver…but there's another singing group that goes by the name of the Rolling Stones. And they got this tune titled, 'You Can't Always Get What You Want….' "

Big Dan smiled at me, and I smiled back. He shook my hand knowingly and settled back on the ER stretcher. I walked back to the desk to fill out the paperwork for the Detox transfer. Big Dan would get a good night's sleep. I would too, knowing that he was safe and sound. Big Dan would get to go home…tomorrow.

# A Little White Candle

I've been tending a little white candle
for the last month and it just taught me
a whole lot about life. It's been some work.
I had to first whittle down the candle's upper-half.
The flame had liquefied the sides and buried the wick.
I carefully dissected the wick free, which then lit
easily. The burning candle at times would extinguish
its flame—overcome by the liquid flow having no path
for escape or able to give space to its source.
Without space or a path the flame died.
I thought how important to tend the flame deep within
our souls that burns and lights our spirit. And then
I thought how important to tend to the flame that burns
in those we love. It takes a lot of work to consciously
tend to a candle. The flames we carry are fragile as
well. We need to honor the space within and the path
our lives take. At the same time, we need to give way
and honor the paths of others. So strike a match and
light a candle. It doesn't take much to light the flame.
Keeping it burning is another story.

 Hands

One morning, years ago, I witnessed a handshake I'll never forget—and learned what hands are really for.

I was an intern working the night shift in the intensive care unit of St. Boniface Hospital in Winnipeg, Canada. The evening began uneventfully. Several patients, all of them stable, didn't command a lot of attention from us that night. The atmosphere was quiet and settled, with a steady hum of monitors and other high-tech gear providing the background noise.

Then came "Mr. Smith," a slim, white-haired man in his early 70s who had suffered a heart attack. At first, he had been admitted to the coronary care unit, where less severely ill patients are generally taken, because his condition was stable. Doctors hoped to treat him conservatively, with no surgical or invasive procedures.

But the damage to his heart was greater than first thought, and he was wheeled into intensive care.

The quiet ended, and a buzz of activity began around Mr. Smith. As his already low blood pressure dropped further, nurses hurriedly inserted more IV lines into his arms. Infusion pumps poured fluids and potent medicines into his veins in an attempt to slow the free fall. After a brief and direct discussion about his condition, he was placed on a ventilator to protect his lungs from being flooded with fluid backing up from his ailing heart. Mr. Smith was now unable to talk. Despite the plastic tube invading his throat and the multiple IV lines tethered to his arms, he could nod and acknowledge how he was doing.

As his family anxiously waited just outside, the medical resident and I watched Mr. Smith closely throughout the night. We readjusted ventilator settings constantly to maximize his breathing and air exchange. Blood drawn hourly documented abnormal body chemistry that worsened to a critical level. Monitors metered his vital signs. Every few minutes, his heartbeats stuttered with sinister rhythms, setting off alarms.

Throughout it all, Mr. Smith was calm and settled, seemingly oblivious to the blares and hisses of the ventilator, the blood draws and other interruptions. "How are you doing?" I'd ask often. Almost imperceptibly, he would nod that he was doing OK. Fleeting glances and silent stares among staff expressed what we all knew to be true, but was left unspoken. Mr. Smith was not in pain and survived until our morning rounds.

The night was very long, but as the hours passed, outside the window the sky began to gradually lighten.

We reported what had transpired and I reviewed Mr. Smith's downward course with Dr. Bruce Light, who was in charge of the intensive care unit, and was just coming on duty. The conclusion was clear: the battle was over. It fell to Dr. Light to share the inevitable prognosis with Mr. Smith. Most patients in Mr. Smith's condition are unconscious from their illness or from medications given to relieve suffering. Mr. Smith was alert and coping the best he could. We all gathered by his bedside.

Dr. Light moved next to Mr. Smith on the right side of the bed. "Mr. Smith, you've suffered a very bad heart attack, and your heart has been severely damaged." Mr. Smith opened his eyes. "Throughout the night we've tried all these medicines that could possibly help, but there's been too much injury to the heart. There isn't anything else we can do." Then he paused. A moment or two passed with their eyes still locked on each other. "Do you understand what I'm saying?" Mr. Smith nodded.

Another moment or two passed.

Very slowly, Mr. Smith raised his right arm and with it all the accompanying plastic tubing. He offered his hand to Dr. Light, who embraced it with his own. They both held on for seconds that were minutes long, and then let go. Dr. Light turned away with tears. The sanctity of the moment permeated the core of everyone by the bedside. I stood in profound reverence in the silence that remained.

Some time later, the IV lines were pumped with a final barrage of medicines to buy as much time as possible. The ventilator tube was removed so Mr. Smith could speak with his family. The IV lines were stopped and monitors shut off. Mr. Smith had a few minutes before he gradually weakened to the point of unconsciousness and died.

Mr. Smith reaching up and offering his hand to Dr. Light in the face of his impending death taught me what hands are really for. Hands are part of how we communicate, connect, and care for one another. They teach us that life is really just about holding on—and letting go.

Mr. Smith knew how to let go. The rest of us just stood there—holding on.

About the Author

Born in Winnipeg, Manitoba, Joel Carter currently practices life and emergency medicine in Duluth, Minnesota. His soul continues to unfold in the good company of friends and family, under the watchful gaze of his four-leggeds and the Silent Ones.